300 Vocabulary Picture Flashcards

English - Persian

granddaughter

نوه

grandmother

مادر بزرگ

grandson

نوه پسر

mother

مادر

nephew

پسر خواهر یا برادر

niece

دختر برادر یا خواهر و غیره

sister

خواهر

son

فرزند پسر

stepdaughter

ناپدری

stepmother

مادر خوانده

stepson

پسر خوانده

uncle

عمو یا دایی

bowl

کاسه

cup

فنجان

dish

ظرف

fork

چنگال

glass

شیشه

knife

چاقو

mug

لیوان

napkin

دستمال

pepper

فلفل

pitcher

پارچ

plate

بشقاب

salad

سالاد

salt

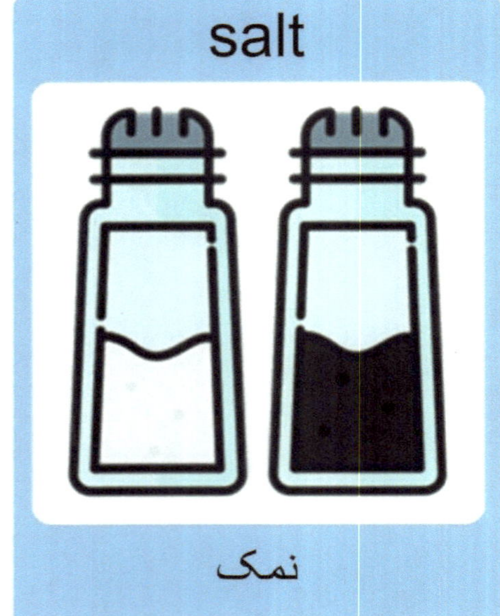

نمک

saucer

نعلبکی

spoon

قاشق

sugar	Sunday	Monday
	Sunday	Monday
قند	یکشنبه	دوشنبه

Tuesday	Wednesday	Thursday
Tuesday	Wednesday	Thursday
سه‌شنبه	چهار شنبه	پنج شنبه

Friday	Saturday	bake
Friday	Saturday	
جمعه	شنبه	پخت

boil	broil	can opener

جوشیدن	برنج	در بازکن

fry	grill	measuring cup

سرخ کردن	کوره	جام اندازه گیری

measuring spoon	microwave	mixing bowl

قاشق اندازه گیری	مایکروویو	کاسه مخلوط کردن

paper towels	poach	potholder

دستمال توالت	طعم دهنده تخم مرغ	نگهدارنده گلدان

roast	rolling pin	scramble

کباب	غلتک	تقلا کردن

simmer	knife	spoon

بجوش	چاقو	قاشق

spatula

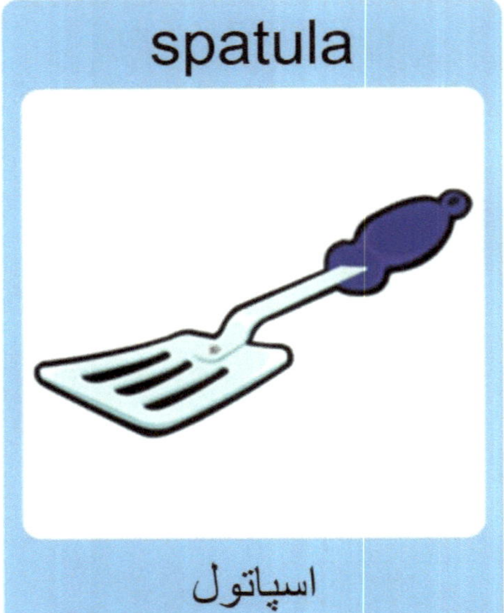

اسپاتول

steam

بخار

strainer

صاف کننده

timer

تایمر

fork

چنگال

toaster

توستر

kettle

کتری

refrigerator

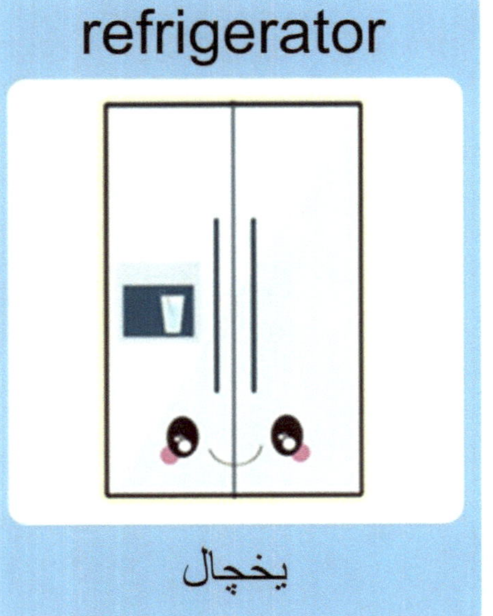

یخچال

blender

مخلوط کن

cabinet	cupboard	microwave

کابینت	کابینت	مایکروویو

back	cheeks	chest

بازگشت	گونه ها	سینه

chin	ears	eyebrows
	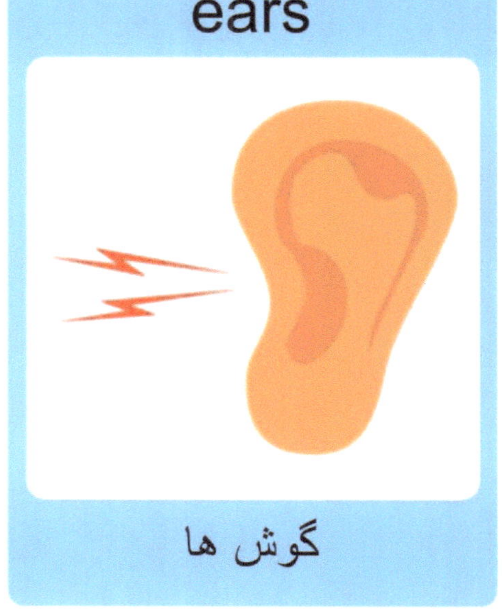	
چانه	گوش ها	ابرو

eyes	feet	fingers

چشم ها	پا	انگشتان

foot	forehead	hair

پا	پیشانی	مو

hands	head	hips
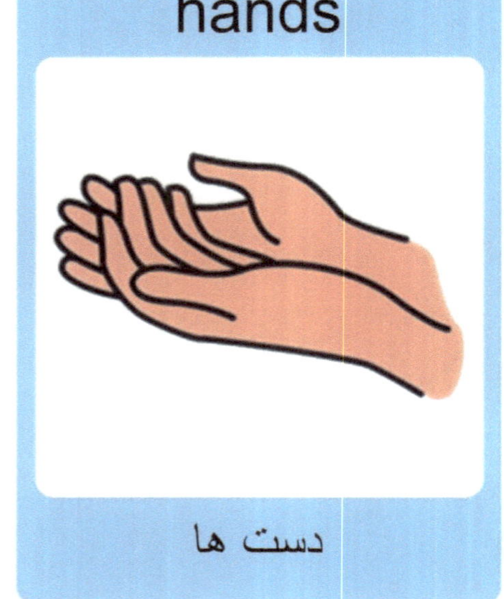		
دست ها	سر	باسن

knees	legs	lips

زانو	پاها	لب

mouth	neck	nose
		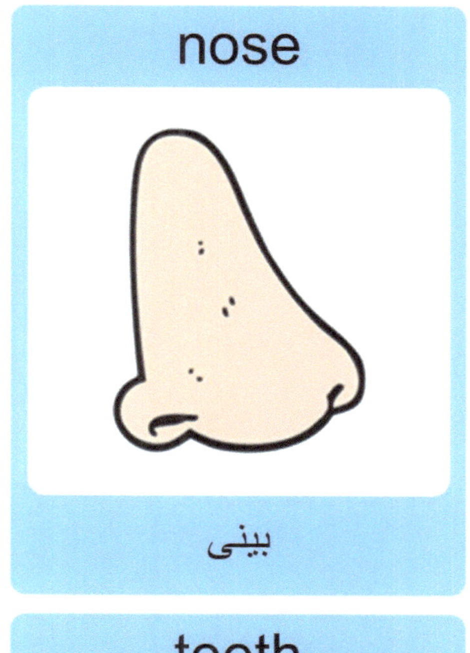
دهان	گردن	بینی

shoulders	stomach	teeth
		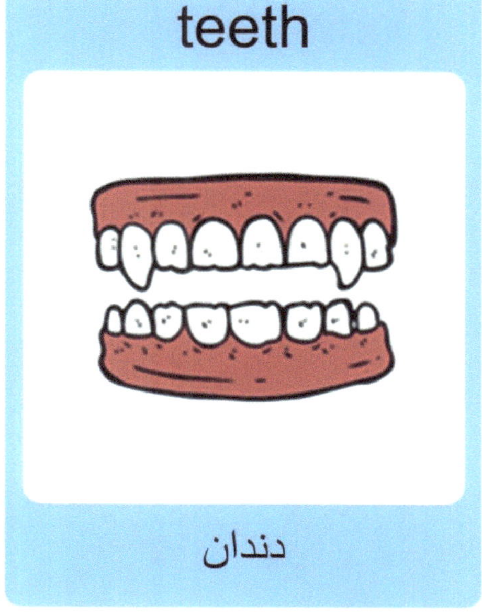
شانه ها	معده	دندان

throat

گلو

toes

انگشتان پا

tongue
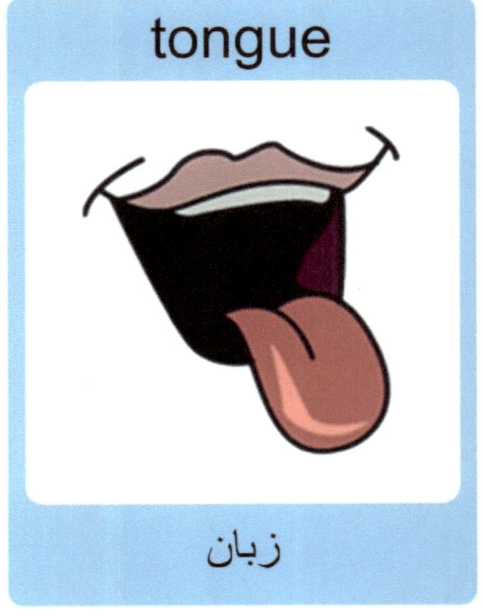
زبان

tooth
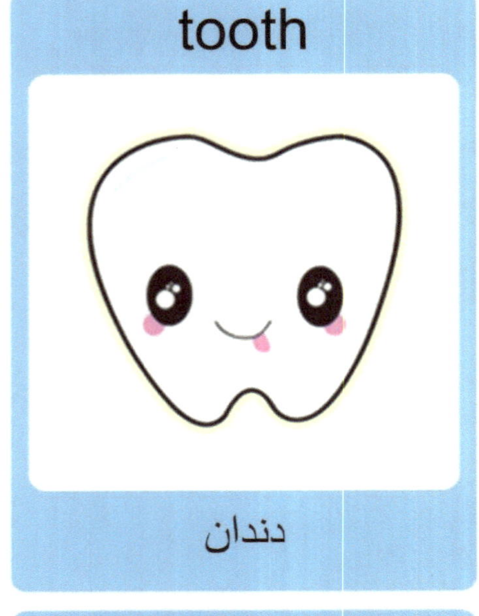
دندان

waist

کمر

overalls

لباس

mittens
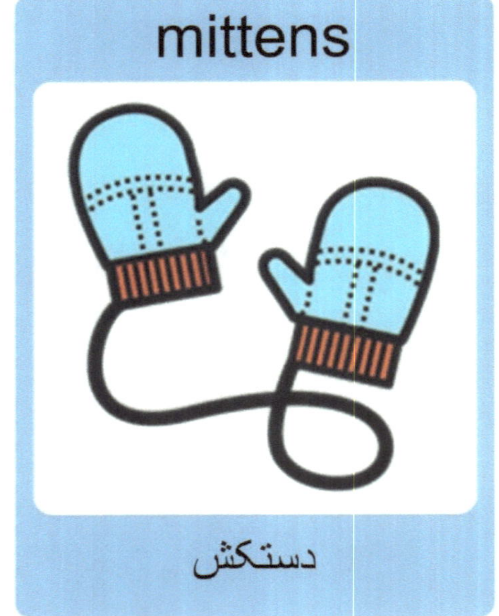
دستکش

beanie

بانی

apron

پیشبند

doll	rattle	toy

عروسک	تکان خوردن	اسباب بازی

diaper	bassinet	bib

پوشک	باسینت	بی بی

octagon	triangle	square
		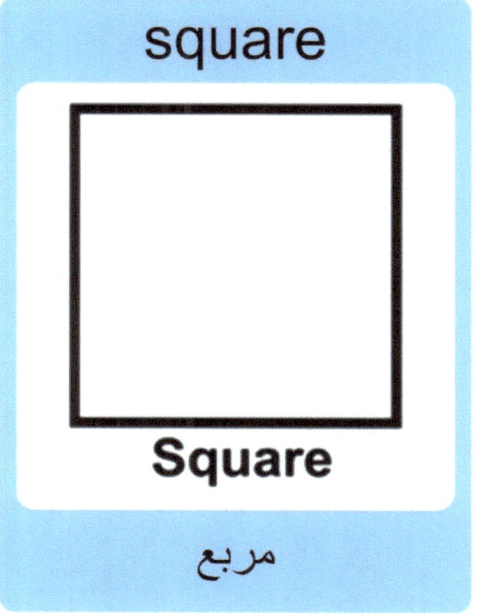
هشت وجهی	مثلث	مربع

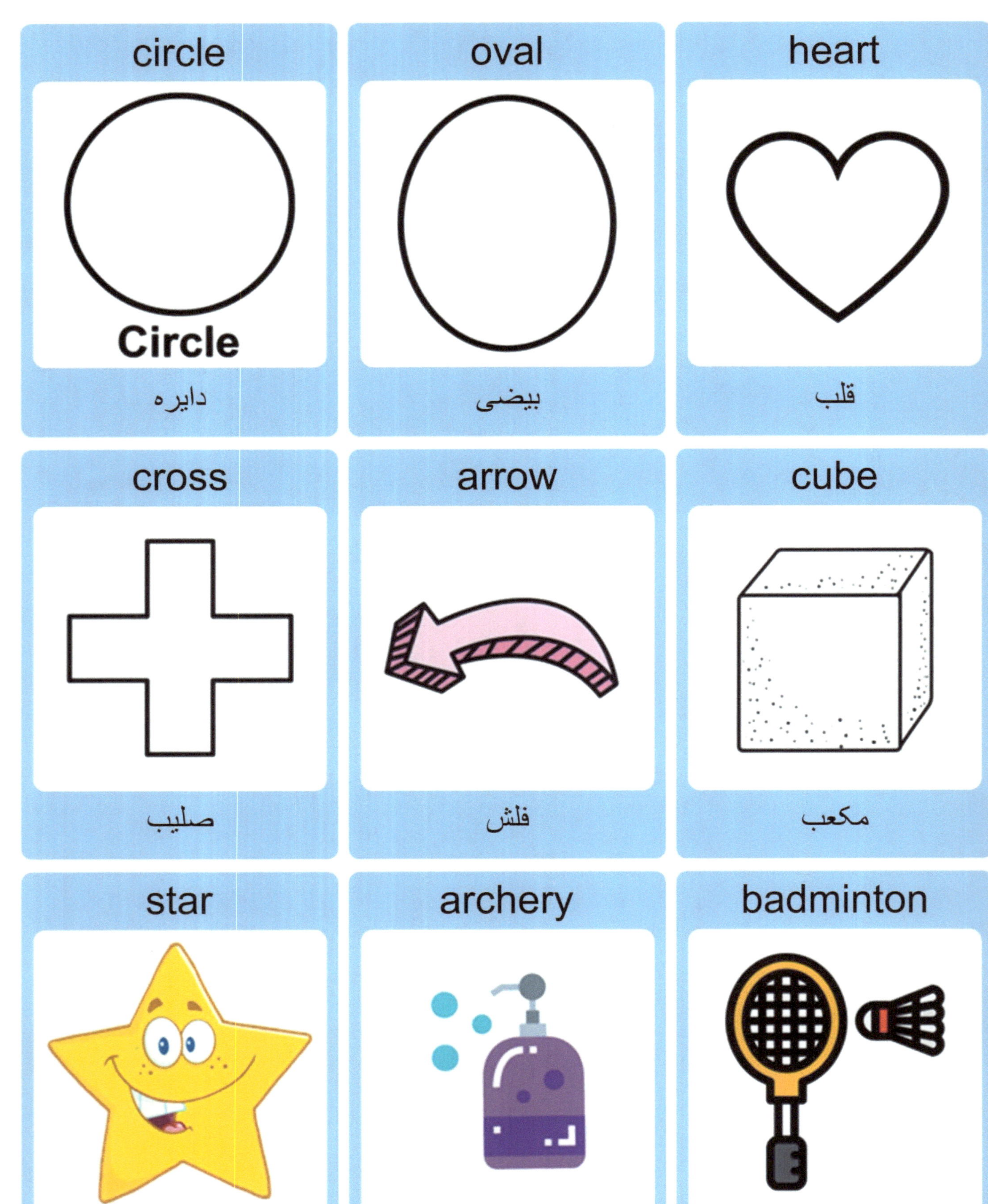

circle
Circle
دایره

oval
بیضی

heart
قلب

cross
صلیب

arrow
فلش

cube
مکعب

star
ستاره

archery
تیراندازی با کمان

badminton
بدمینتون

cricket

کریکت

bowling

بولینگ

boxing

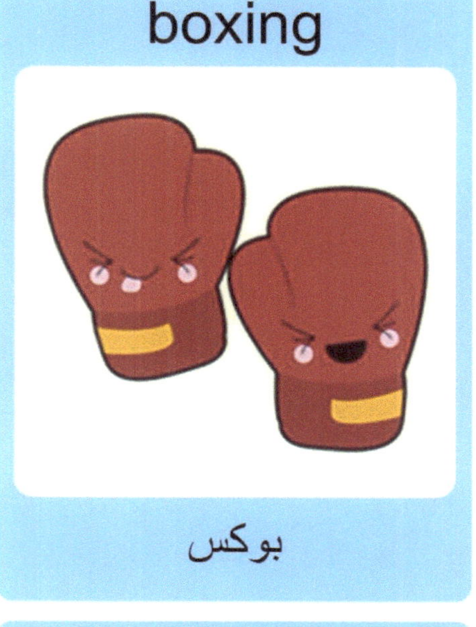

بوکس

tennis

تنیس

skateboarding

ورزش اسکیت بورد

surfing

تخته موج سواری

hockey

هاکی

yoga

یوگا

fencing

شمشیر بازی

fitness	gymnastics	karate

تناسب اندام	ژیمناستیک	کاراته
volleyball	weightlifting	basketball

والیبال	وزنه برداری	بسکتبال
baseball	rugby	wrestling
	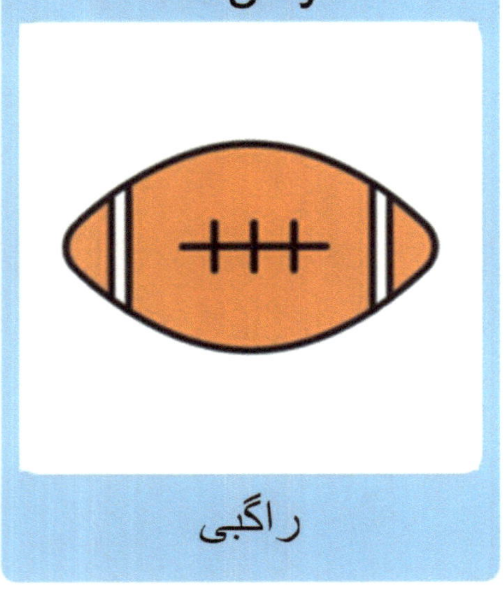	
بیسبال	راگبی	کشتی

car racing

مسابقات اتومبیل رانی

cycling

دوچرخه سواري

running

در حال دویدن

table tennis

تنیس روی میز

fishing

صید ماهی

judo

جودو

climbing

سنگ نوردی

shooting

تیراندازی کردن

golf

گلف

ride	sit down	stand up

سوار شوید	بنشین	بایستید

fight	laugh	read

مبارزه کردن	خنده	خواندن

play	listen	cry

بازی	گوش کنید	گریه کردن

think

فکر

sing

آواز خواندن

watch tv

تلویزیون را تماشا کنید

dance

رقص

turn on

روشن کن

turn off

خاموش کنید

win

پیروزی

fly

پرواز

cut

قطع کردن

throw away	sleep	close

دور انداختن	خواب	نزدیک

open	write	give

باز کن	نوشتن	دادن

jump	eat	drink

پرش	بخور	بنوش

cook

پختن

wash

شستشو

wait

صبر کن

climb

بالا رفتن

talk

صحبت

crawl

خزیدن

dream

رویا

dig

حفر کردن

clap

کف زدن

knit

بافتن

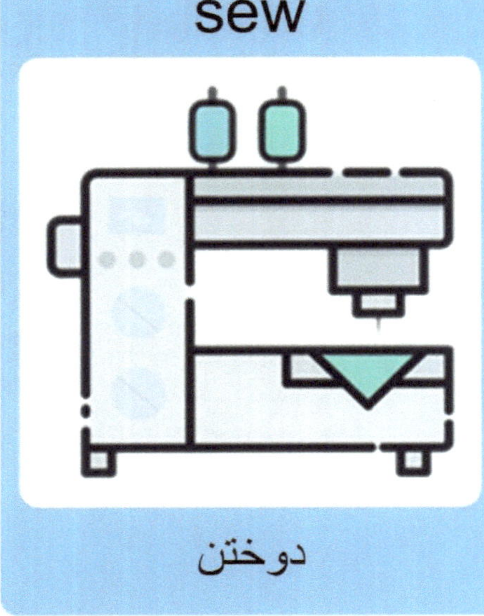

sew

دوختن

smell

بو

kiss

بوسه

hug

در آغوش گرفتن

snore

خروپف

bathe

حمام کردن

bow

رکوع

paint

رنگ

dive

شیرجه رفتن

ski

اسکی

stack

پشته

buy

خرید

shake

تکان دادن

programmer

برنامه نویس

veterinarian

دامپزشکی

street vendor

فروشنده خیابانی

miner

معدن کار

teacher	bellboy	speaker

معلم	باربر، پیشخدمت	بلندگو
butcher	pharmacist	receptionist

قصاب	داروساز	مسئول پذیرش
politician	tour guide	entrepreneur

سیاستمدار	راهنمای تور	کارآفرین

ballet dancer
رقصنده باله

astronaut
فضانورد

judge
قاضی

lawyer
وکیل

cashier
صندوقدار

taxi driver
راننده تاکسی

plumber
لوله کش

musician
نوازنده

chef
سرآشپز

baker

بیکر

artist

هنرمند

actor

بازیگر

bartender

پارس

hairdresser

آرایشگاه

bishop

اسقفها

optician

عینک فروشی

florist

گلدار

writer

نویسنده

accountant	wine	coffee

حسابدار	شراب	قهوه
lemonade	hot chocolate	milkshake

لیموناد	شکلات داغ	میلکشیک
water	tea	milk

اب	چای	شیر

beer

آبجو

soda

جوش شیرین

smoothie

اسموتی

milkshake

میلکشیک

coconut milk

شیر نارگیل

orange juice

آب پرتقال

cocoa

کاکائو

cheese

پنیر

egg

تخم مرغ

butter

کره

margarine

مارگارین

yogurt

ماست

cottage cheese

پنیر کلم

ice cream

بستنی

cream

کرم رنگ

sandwich

ساندویچ

sausage

سوسیس

hamburger

همبرگر

hot dog

هات داگ

bread

نان

pizza

پیتزا

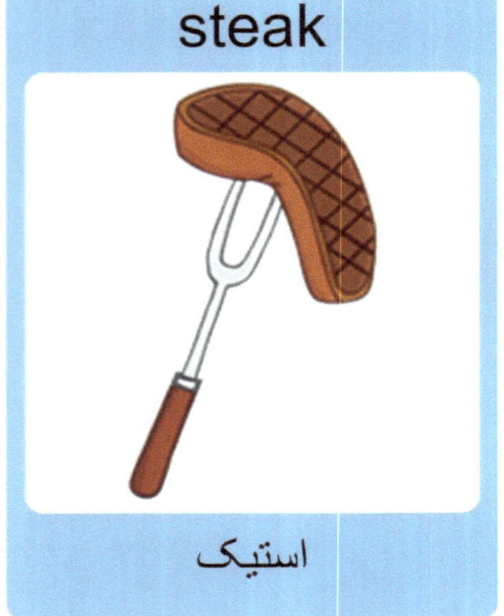

steak

استیک

roast chicken

مرغ سرخ شده

fish

ماهی

seafood

غذای دریایی

ham

ژامبون

kebab

کباب

bacon	sour cream	cow

بیکن	خامه ترش	گاو

rabbit	duck	shrimp

خرگوش	اردک	میگو

pig	bee	goat

خوک	زنبور عسل	بز

crab	deer	turkey

خرچنگ	گوزن	بوقلمون

dove	sheep	fish

کبوتر	گوسفند	ماهی

chicken	horse	wing chair

جوجه	اسب	صندلی

tv stand	sofa	cushion

میز تلویزیون	کاناپه	کوسن ها

telephone	television	speaker

تلفن	تلویزیون	بلندگوها

end table	tea set	fireplace

میز کناری	سرویس چای خوری	بخاری

remote

از راه دور

fan

پنکه برقی

floor lamp

چراغ پایهدار

carpet

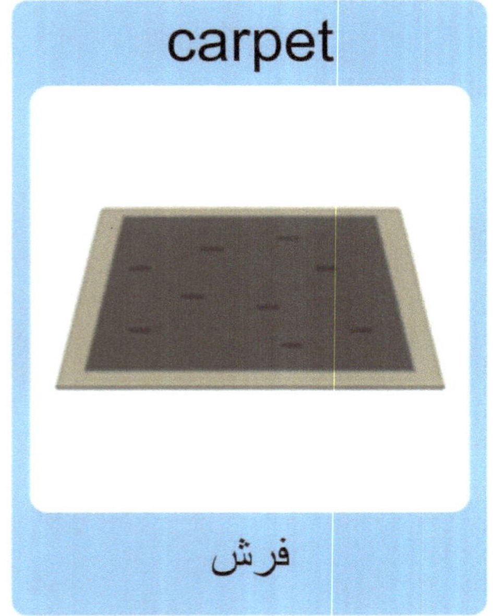

فرش

table

میز

blinds

پرده

curtains

پرده ها

picture

تصویر

vase

گلدان

clock

ساعت

pillow

بالش

hat stand

چوب لباسی

dressing table

میز رختکن

table lamp

لامپ میز

mirror

آینه

ironing board

تخته اتو

hope chest

جعبه با کشو

night table

میز کنار تخت

bed

بستر

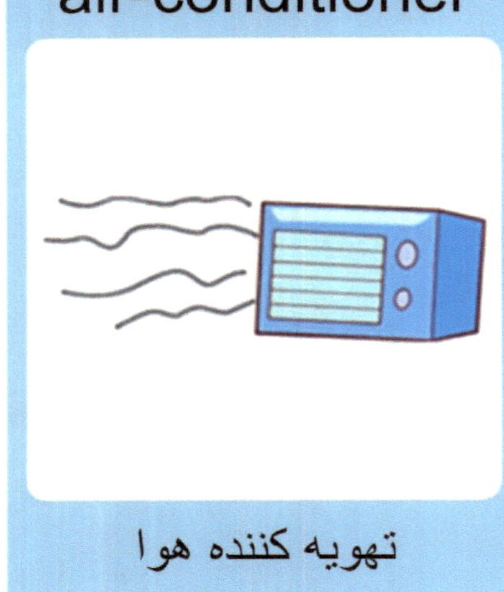

air-conditioner

تهویه کننده هوا

jug

کوزه

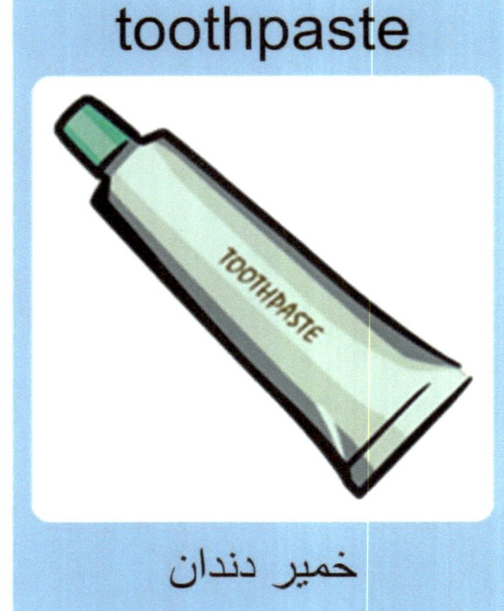

toothpaste

خمیر دندان

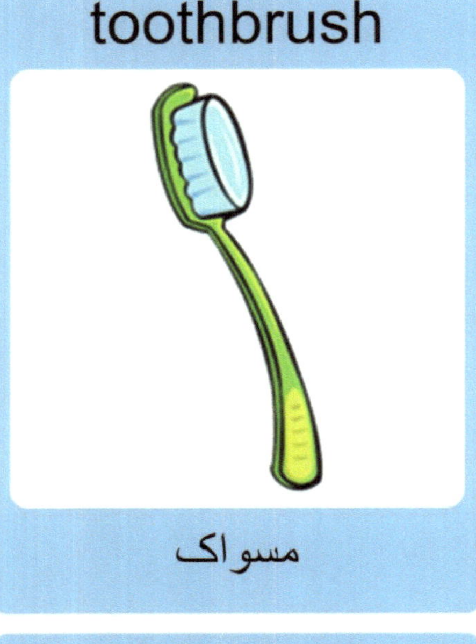

toothbrush

مسواک

soap

صابون

clothespin

لباس

hanger

جا رختی

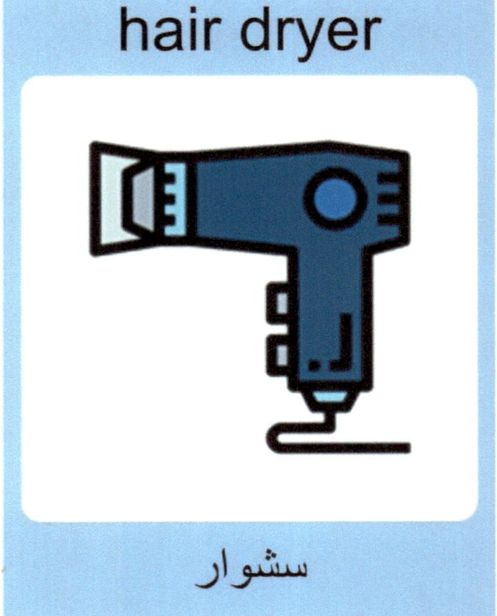

hair dryer

سشوار

shampoo

شامپو

bubble

حباب

brush

قلم مو

toilet paper

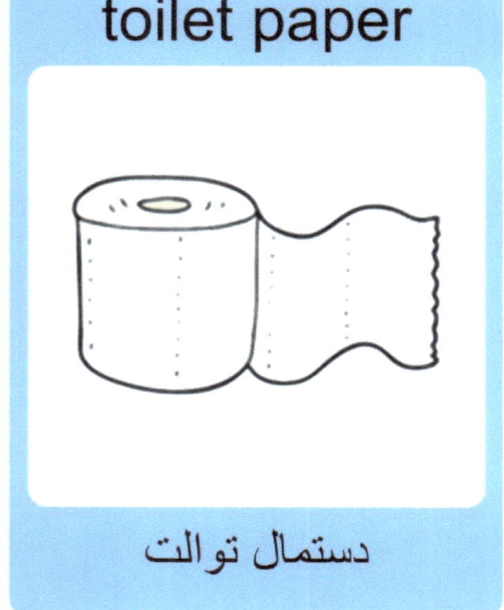

دستمال توالت

towel

حوله

clothesline

خط لباس

shower

دوش

bathtub

وان

laundry detergent

پودر لباس شویی

bucket

سطل

mops

مپس

liquid soap

صابون مایع

washing powder

پودر شستشو

trash bag

کیسه زباله

trash can

سطل آشغال

sinks

غرق می شود

toilet bowl

کاسه توالت

washing machine

ماشین لباسشویی

laundry basket

سبد لباسشویی

razor

تیغ

electric razor

تیغ برقی

shaving cream

کرم اصلاح

mouthwash

دهانشویه

cotton bud

جوانه پنبه

hair brush

برس مو

comb

شانه

cleanser

پاک کننده